PENGUIN BOOKS

THE MAKING OF RED DWARF

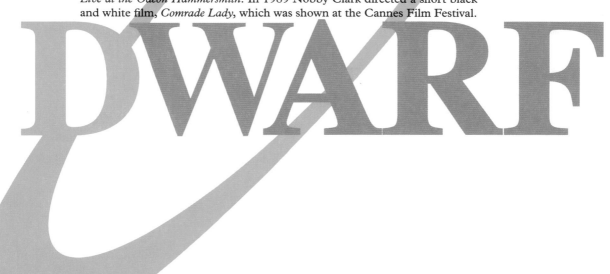

JOE NAZZARO was born and educated in New Jersey, and gained his BA at Scranton University, Pennsylvania. His interest in science fiction began at an early age when he was adopted by a Dalek in Central Park. Now able to cruise the universe, he began to write regularly for magazines on both sides of the Atlantic. His first book, examining the alien make-up of *Star Trek: The Next Generation*, was published in 1992. He is married to a British make-up artist, and has adopted two budgies who are teaching him to fly in order to reduce the cost of air fares between the US and the UK.

NOBBY CLARK is one of this country's leading photographers. He began his career at Michael Croft's National Youth Theatre in 1968 and from there went on to take photographs for various fringe venues, including the Soho Poly and Bush Theatre. He has now worked for all the major subsidized theatres, opera and ballet companies, and also for many West End productions. He has received commissions from the *Observer*, the *Guardian*, *The Times* and the *Sunday Times*, and has worked in television and film for many directors, including David Hare, John Schlesinger and Richard Eyre. In 1987 he directed the No. 1 bestselling video *Billy and Albert* of Billy Connolly live in concert at the Albert Hall, and this led to another bestselling video in 1991, *Billy Connolly Live at the Odeon Hammersmith*. In 1989 Nobby Clark directed a short black and white film, *Comrade Lady*, which was shown at the Cannes Film Festival.

JOE NAZZARO

THE MAKING OF RED DWARF

PENGUIN BOOKS

PENGUIN BOOKS

Published by the Penguin Group
Penguin Books Ltd, 27 Wrights Lane, London W8 5TZ, England
Penguin Books USA Inc., 375 Hudson Street, New York, New York 10014, USA
Penguin Books Australia Ltd, Ringwood, Victoria, Australia
Penguin Books Canada Ltd, 10 Alcorn Avenue, Toronto, Ontario, Canada M4V 3B2
Penguin Books (NZ) Ltd, 182–190 Wairau Road, Auckland 10, New Zealand

Penguin Books Ltd, Registered Offices: Harmondsworth, Middlesex, England

First published 1994
10 9 8 7 6 5 4 3 2 1

Filmset in Monotype Plantin by Selwood Systems, Midsomer Norton

Printed and bound in Great Britain by Butler & Tanner Ltd, Frome and London

For Rose Nazzaro,
who taught me the value of wurds

CONTENTS

ACKNOWLEDGEMENTS

It would have been impossible to write a 'Making Of' book without the help of the many talented people who work on *Red Dwarf*. Special thanks to: Helen, who sent that first fax; Bridget and Cressida, for getting me there and back; Justin, who taught me a new phrase: 'I have no problem with that'; Mel, who I hope will show me how to do that bar trick with the foil; Ron and Jackie, for their taste in wine; Dai, for letting me make fun of his ear-ring; Rocket, for telling me how he got his nickname; Peter Wragg and the gang, for letting me hang out with them; Danny, who's great to do a convention with; Chris, who let down his guard occasionally; John and Jeff, for the chips; Andria, Lois and Annie, because I have a soft spot for make-up artists; Terry and Karl, for their glimpse of tomorrow's technology; Howard G. and Graham, for the long phone interviews; everyone at the Laredo Western Club who asked me 'Does it look like the real thing?'; Nobby, for his brilliant work; and of course Rob and Doug who provided grist for the mill.

Finally, I'd like to thank the person who helped me every step of the way on this project, in more ways than I could possibly count. To Sheelagh Wells, I offer my undying gratitude. This book is hers too.

Joe Nazzaro

FOREWORD

Joe,

For the last time, we have absolutely no intention of writing a foreword for your damned book, *Red Dwarf . . . The Making of*. Yes, it may be well-written and informative, and give many intriguing insights into how the show is translated from page to screen. OK, it features dozens of exciting exclusive photographs in full colour. But if you think we're giving you one nanosecond of our time to help you make parasitic bucks on the back of our awesome, no, bigger than awesome . . . no, even bigger than bigger than awesome talent, then you're sadly mistaken, Bucko.

Still, now that your book has not got a foreword written by us, almost certainly no one will buy it, meaning you have wasted four months of your miserable life trailing the *Red Dwarf* crew around, asking annoying questions, and almost certainly you will end up in some gutter somewhere, croaking pathetically about how you once met the real Craig Charles in actual person, as you suck on a can of extra-strong wino-type lager.

So leap, little flea, on to some other lumbering talent and suck that dry.

Best wishes,

GRANT NAYLOR

PS By the way, we took your advice about attending those assertion classes. Cheers.

PROLOGUE

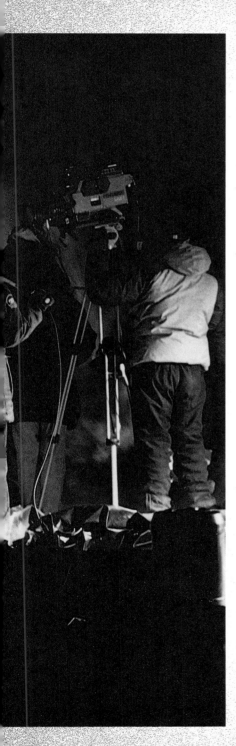

Late night on the docks. The fog has started to roll in, covering the ground with thick clouds of cloying mist. The city is unknown; Chicago maybe, or New York, or Philadelphia's South Street; it's not important. In the distance a bell sounds a mournful refrain, and tiny waves beat quietly against wood and steel.

From somewhere in the fog the staccato sound of footsteps grows louder until, without warning, the clouds of mist part, and a woman emerges into the harsh, uncompromising glare of one of the city's ancient streetlights. She drops the two suitcases she has been carrying and stands silently, the light glistening on tiny particles of trapped mist on the fashionable hat and the dress that clings to her slim frame.

A black automobile slides to a halt a few feet away – a '38 Bentley, perhaps a '39 – its windscreen opaque with condensation. A man emerges from its dark interior reaching for a pack of cigarettes as he moves towards her, a wide hat throwing his face into a mask of deep shadows. 'Maybe it's the moonlight,' he whispers, 'but I've got to admit, you're looking pretty good for a corpse.'

In the momentary illumination from a flaring match, we recognize the distinctive features of Dave Lister, the last human being in the universe . . .

So begins 'Gunmen of the Apocalypse', one of the most ambitious and unusual episodes of *Red Dwarf* ever filmed . . .

Chris Barrie returns as Ace Rimmer in *Red Dwarf VI* – what a guy!

INTRODUCTION

In *Red Dwarf VI*, writers/creators Rob Grant and Doug Naylor have made a number of significant changes to their winning formula. The most obvious difference in the new series is the absence of Red Dwarf itself, which was stolen somewhere between series five and six. This year, the action takes place in the smaller, more mobile ship-to-surface transport craft Starbug.

The loss of Red Dwarf also meant that Holly, the ship's computer with a senile CPU, had to be written out of season VI. Without Hattie Hayridge who plays Holly, a greater emphasis has now been placed on the remaining four characters.

'We wanted to take the series in a different direction, giving it a new energy,' explains Doug. 'We felt if the crew were forced into a much smaller craft, with low supplies, it would give a fresh new edge to the series. Obviously, you don't know in advance if it's going to work, but we had to make the decision quite early on, to say, "OK, Red Dwarf is out." To that extent I think it's given the series a different feel. It's back to basics – this time round they're thrown on their mettle. The Universe is a much more vicious place in season VI.'

'In season V,' continues Rob, 'we felt the stories set

aboard Starbug had a grittier tone and texture. When the crew were more hands-on and in control, for us those shows were more exciting. It's the difference between being marooned at sea and getting tossed about in a little dinghy, or being stuck on a fully-stocked deserted ocean liner. On Starbug, the danger is more in-your-face.

'We thought long and hard about the decision to "rest" Holly. We always make an effort to try and move the characters along every season. We felt, and it was also reflected in the fan opinion we were getting, that we were under-using Holly and the Cat. We thought by losing one of them from the equation, at least temporarily, the function of the remaining four would be enhanced, and I feel that has worked. The balance has been split more evenly in the sixth series.'

'The Cat has a more integrated role this time out,' says Doug. 'He's become a functioning member of the team; piloting Starbug, and acting as an early-warning system thanks to his awesomely-talented nose. His sense of smell has developed to the point where he can literally smell danger from a mile off.'

Another major character development in the sixth season is Rimmer's new hard light mode, which gives him the power of touch. The idea was originally only intended for 'Legion', the second episode, but the writers felt it was too good to waste, and carried it into later stories as well. 'When we made the decision to give Rimmer a hard light drive,' notes Rob, 'it was a function of the initial plot. We intended to return to the *status quo ante* at the end of that story, but it was such a tempting idea to give Rimmer a physical presence when he needed one, we kept going back to it.'

Not all changes in *Red Dwarf VI* have been made in

front of the camera. In order to meet the challenges of their most ambitious series yet, Rob and Doug added two new members to their team: director Andy DeEmmony, whose extensive work on *Spitting Image* gave him a good working knowledge of studio-bound special effects, and producer Justin Judd who had just worked with Rob and Doug on the pilot show of their upcoming Carlton TV series, *The 10%ers*.

As one of the new faces on *Red Dwarf*, Justin found it a bit daunting at first, producing a well-known series with a crew that had been together for several years. 'It is difficult. There are two elements that must be dealt with: how do you make your mark creatively on a show whose formula is already well established, and as the producer you're also responsible for telling people who know the show much better than you how things should be done logistically.

Two of the new faces on *Red Dwarf VI* : producer Justin Judd (*above*) and director Andy DeEmmony (*left*)

It's a question of making your mark early on. You have to show you know what you are talking about, but you also must show that you know the programme. It's a gradual process.'

For Andy, who had to hit the ground running as the new director, there were a few problems that had to be solved fairly quickly. 'I suppose the hardest thing for me was to get a handle on the difference between reality and slapstick. On *Spitting Image* the temptation for me, visually, is: if you see a bit of business that can get a laugh, you go for it, because you want to increase the density of laughs. With *Red Dwarf*, everything has to be played very believably, very straight. Instead of playing for the laugh, we play it a little low and ride the jokes off it, rather than asking for them. I've enjoyed working that way and it's much more satisfying than the "where's my laugh?" approach which a lot of sitcoms use. But then, *Red Dwarf* isn't exactly like "a lot of sitcoms".'

In season VI, the creative team has put together one of the most diverse and compelling group of episodes yet. The series opens with 'Psirens', a fast moving adventure, drawing on elements of Greek mythology, followed by 'Legion', in which the Red Dwarf crew encounters a mysterious masked being, who may be a genius, a saint, or a force of unspeakable evil.

The third episode is 'Gunmen of the Apocalypse', which blends film noir with science fiction and spaghetti westerns. Fourth is 'Rimmerworld', where the crew discovers that one Rimmer is more than enough. 'Polymorph II: Emohawk', a real crowd-pleaser, features the return of Rimmer's and the Cat's celebrated *alter egos*: Ace 'Smoke me a kipper' Rimmer and Duane 'Suck my thermos' Dibbley, as well as a shape-changing creature similar to

Vis-fx assistant Paul McGuiness helps bring the title creature to life in Polymorph II: Emohawk

one the crew faced way back in season III. The season
ends with 'Out of Time', when the boys from *Red Dwarf*
meet their future selves, and are appalled by what they are
destined to become.

To show how an episode of *Red Dwarf* is produced, we will
now follow one story from beginning to end, starting from
the conception of the initial idea, through rehearsals and
shooting, and finally into the post-production process.

'Gunmen of the Apocalypse' was a particular favourite
for the cast and crew, and one of the most technically
complex *Red Dwarf* stories to date.

Craig Charles: ' "Gunmen" was great. In that episode I got to kiss a girl, fire a gun, and dress up as a cowboy. Not only that – I got paid!'

Chris Barrie: 'I was nervous at first, but the longer I was on the horse, the better it was. Apart from when Craig shouted "Yee-hah!" at the end, and I nearly went into the back of the stagecoach.'

In addition to the black and white gangster sequence that opens the story, 'Gunmen' also features rogue Simulants, an explosive space battle, a runaway computer virus, the Vindalooian ambassador, a western gunfight between a drunken mechanoid sheriff and the Four Horsemen of the Apocalypse, a boiling lava planet, and the most unusual bar fight staged for *Red Dwarf* since the third season episode, 'Backwards'.

To get an idea of how much blood, sweat and expletives go into translating the show from concept to screen, this book charts the making of 'Gunmen of the Apocalypse' from start to finish, before its autumn launch on BBC2.

As with every episode of *Red Dwarf*, 'Gunmen of the Apocalypse' started with an idea...

THE STORY

For Rob Grant and Doug Naylor, the story behind 'Gunmen of the Apocalypse' started with a simple premise: they wanted to write a western. 'We both thought a western theme could provide the basis for a wonderful *Red Dwarf* episode,' recalls Doug, 'but with our producers' hats on, we didn't want to start writing it until we were sure it could be shot convincingly, which meant finding an authentic western town, preferably in the Shepperton/Chertsey area, and then getting a budget done to see if we could afford the horses and the entire kit and caboodle that comes with doing a western.'

As luck would have it, the new director, Andy DeEmmony, vaguely recalled hearing of two western 'towns'; one in Kent, and the other somewhere near Birmingham. 'He went off on a recce,' continues Rob, 'and returned with some camcorder footage of the Laredo Western Club, in Kent. Laredo is an actual town that western devotees have built for themselves as a copy of an authentic frontier town. They've built their own little shacks at the back of each storefront, and they actually spend weekends living there in cowboy style. They fine each other for smoking pre-rolled modern cigarettes, and wearing watches, and they try to live as authentically as possible.'

Doug: 'We played the tape and thought, hey, it looks pretty good. There were also club members available as extras who had their own authentic costumes, guns and horses, and bad teeth, so in terms of cost it suddenly started looking feasible to make what we started to call the first "Roast Beef" western.'

With a realistic location available, Rob and Doug no longer had an excuse not to come up with a story. They started by immersing themselves in the genre, to see what had been done before, what worked and what to avoid. 'We watched an amazing amount of westerns!' notes Doug, 'including *The Searchers, Stagecoach, Rio Bravo*, lots of John Wayne and Clint Eastwood, and all the Howard Hawks and John Ford material. We really tried to absorb as much of the genre as we could.

'From the beginning, we had an image we really liked, of Kryten being some kind of sheriff, but at this point we didn't know why, or indeed what our starting point would be. When we write a script, we plot it meticulously, doing scene breakdowns from beginning to end, and don't actually start writing it until the story is completely mapped out. With this particular episode, we threw the rule book out of the window and plunged right into the western section, not knowing why the characters were there or what it was all about.'

'One thing we tried to avoid,' says Rob, 'was repeating elements of previous science fiction westerns, or even western clichés in general. We didn't want to do a *Blazing Saddles*-type spoof, because *Blazing Saddles* is a definitive spoof. Equally, we had to avoid problems of bumping up against *Westworld*, or the classic *Star Trek* episode "Shadow of the Gun".'

Another significant difference in the early drafts of

'Gunmen' was that Rob and Doug wanted to shoot the exterior scenes at night. 'From a visual standpoint,' explains Doug, 'shooting on tape in England during the day, where the weather is changing every twenty minutes, nearly always looks appalling. If you shoot at night, you can get the lights in there, and between a few blue lights and a bit of smoke, it looks incredibly effective. For that reason, we always assumed the story was going to be *High Noon* or, more accurately, *High Midnight*.'

Red Dwarf writers and co-creators, Doug Naylor (*left*) and Rob Grant

Half-way through the writing process, Rob and Doug decided to check out the Laredo Western Village to get a better idea of what the location looked like, and how it could be shot. The trip was an eye-opener, to say the least. 'We went to Laredo, along with Andy and a few members of the production team,' remembers Doug, 'and the village was over two feet deep in mud! The weather had been absolutely foul, and we thought: It's impossible to shoot here. The cameras can't rest on this ground, and people won't be able to walk from point A to point B. The horses will churn up the mud and it will be incredibly difficult, especially at night. At that point the whole thing took a dive and we seriously considered aborting the whole show.'

'I remember a few of the club members were there to show us around,' adds Rob, 'and one of them decided to demonstrate his gun in a very confined room, where Justin and a few of the team were milling around. The man drew his gun without warning and shot it off right next to Justin's head. He suffered partial deafness in one ear, right through to post-production. As a result, he had a thoroughly miserable time during the shoot and has now developed a pathological fear of cowboys.'

Despite their misgivings, they went back to work on the 'Gunmen' script. After working backwards from their western premise, they came up with the idea of Kryten contracting a computer virus, and built the story's science fiction framework around it. The script was handed in, and the production team began discussing the potential problems involved in shooting it.

Rob: 'At one of the early planning meetings, the opinion from the various departments was that it was at least a two day shoot, possibly three. In fact, Rocket, our head cameraman, at one point was recommending five days. All of which made it prohibitively expensive. To Andy's credit, he backed us up, and said "Yes, I think we can shoot this in one night, provided nothing goes wrong." '

Almost immediately, something went wrong. For economic reasons, the night shoot had to be cancelled. According to Doug, 'It turned out that Kent was just outside the area considered to be a London studio, which meant the entire production team would have to be put up in hotels after the shooting finished. That turned out to be fantastically expensive, so the night shoot had to be turned into a day shoot. That worried us a great deal. The chances of getting an absolutely glorious day in the middle of February were very, very remote, but at this point there was no choice. The script had been written, we had looked at other locations and they were no better, so we had to keep with Laredo and pray the weather was good. What kills you, shooting in England is, you get five minutes of sun, then it goes cloudy, and then it rains, which is what happens whenever we go shooting. We generally get eight or nine different kinds of weather.'

With the script cut and re-drafted for the fifth time, and a shooting day booked in Laredo, it was time to begin production on 'Gunmen of the Apocalypse', the third episode of *Red Dwarf VI* . . .

THE FIRST ROAST BEEF WESTERN

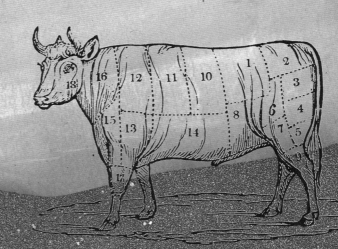

SUNDAY

The *Red Dwarf* sets have been built on Stage G at Shepperton Studios, home of countless films and television projects, including *The Third Man*, *Oliver!*, *Robin Hood: Prince of Thieves* and Mel Gibson's *Hamlet*, for the past three seasons. Scattered amongst the workshops and sound-stages at Shepperton are a number of disused back-lots, which have proved to be a bonanza for the *Red Dwarf* production team. This year, they've already returned to the wooded glade used in last season's 'Terrorform' to shoot exteriors for episode four, 'Rimmerworld', and next week they'll be shooting segments of episode five, 'Emohawk', in a village of wooden huts – a set left behind by the short-lived American series *Covington Cross*.

Right now, there isn't much activity at Shepperton, and *Red Dwarf* is the most visible production. There is a series of Guinness TV commercials being filmed on the neighbouring Stage F, and an American film unit has just started work on a new series of the action-adventure drama *Mac-Gyver*. From time to time, their shooting schedule crosses over a bit of *Red Dwarf* location filming, resulting in many puzzled looks from the American crew, who are unable to

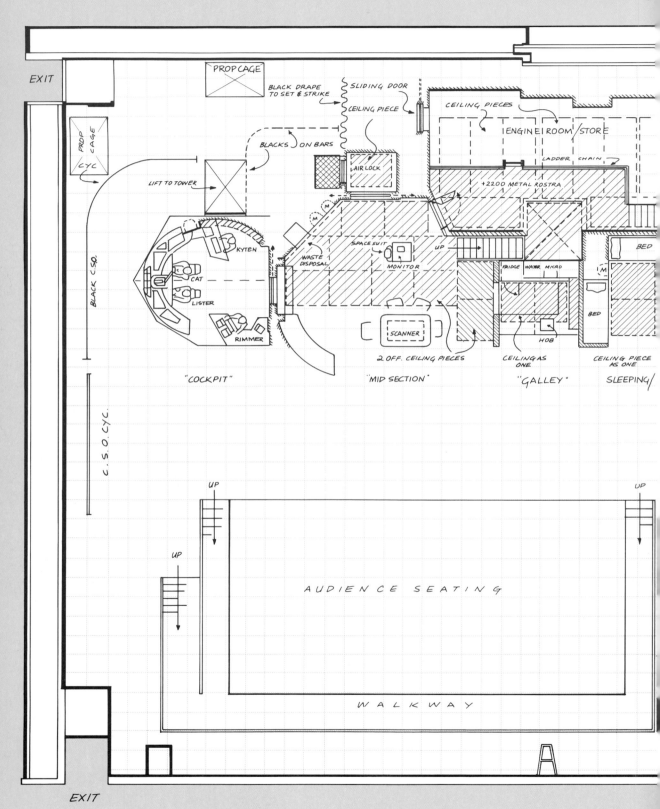

EXIT

PROP CAGE

BLACK DRAPE
TO SET & STRIKE

SLIDING DOOR

CEILING PIECE

CEILING PIECES

ENGINE ROOM / STORE

PROP
CAGE

CYC

BLACKS ON BARS

LADDER CHAIN

LIFT TO TOWER

AIR LOCK

+2200 METAL ROSTRA

M

KYTEN

SPACE SUIT

UP

BED

M

BLACK C.SO.

CAT

WASTE
DISPOSAL

MONITOR

FRIDGE WATER MICRO

LISTER

BED

RIMMER

SCANNER

HOB

C. S. O. CYC.

"COCKPIT"

"MID SECTION"

2 OFF. CEILING PIECES

"GALLEY"

CEILING AS
ONE

CEILING PIECE
AS ONE

SLEEPING

UP

UP

UP

AUDIENCE SEATING

WALKWAY

EXIT

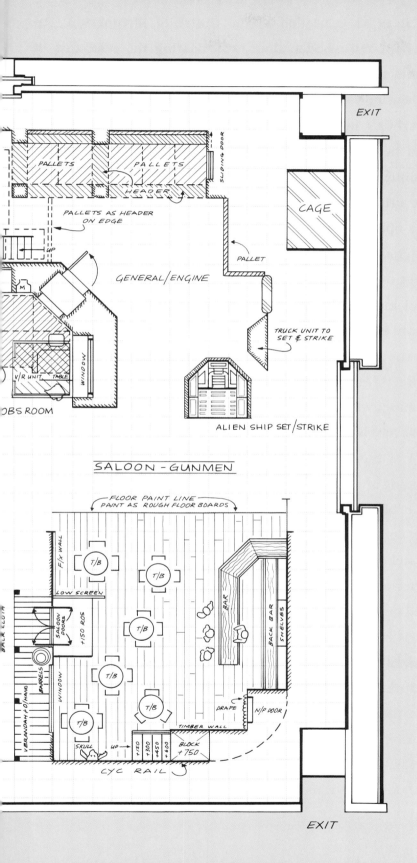

EXIT

PALLETS   PALLETS

HEADER

SLIDING DOOR

CAGE

PALLETS AS HEADER ON EDGE

UP

GENERAL/ENGINE

PALLET

TRUCK UNIT TO SET & STRIKE

M

WINDOW

V/R UNIT   TABLE

OBS ROOM

ALIEN SHIP SET/STRIKE

SALOON - GUNMEN

FLOOR PAINT LINE
PAINT AS ROUGH FLOOR BOARDS

F/X WALL

T/B   T/B

LOW SCREEN

SALOON DOORS

+150 ROS

T/B

BAR

BACK BAR

SHELVES

BACK CLOTH

T/B

WINDOW

T/B

DRAPE

N/P DOOR

VERANDAH + D/HANG

BARRELS

T/B

TIMBER WALL

SKULL   UP   +150   +300   +450   +600   BLOCK +750

CYC RAIL

EXIT

GRANT-NAYLOR MANCHESTER

		DISTRIBUTION
SCALE	1 to 50	
SHEET NO		☐ PRODUCER
NO OF SHEETS		☐ DIRECTOR
DATE DRAWN		☐ DESIGNER
		☐ DESIGN ASST
PRODUCER	JUSTIN JUDD	☐ TECH MANAGER
DIRECTOR	ANDY DE EMMONY	☐ ENG MANAGER
		☐ FLOOR MANAGER
DESIGNER	MEL BIBBY	☐ S S A
DRAWN BY		☐ ESTIMATOR
		☐ CONTRACTOR
ZERO DATE		☐ SCENIC ARTIST
FILM DATE		☐ CARPENTERS
		☐ PAINTERS
V. T. R. DATE		☐ ELECTRICIANS
TRANS. DATE		☐ VISUAL EFFECTS
		☐ METAL WORK
CONTRACTOR		☐ SCENE SUPERVISOR
O. B LOCATION		☐ HOUSE FOREMAN
STUDIO	'G' SHEPPERTON	☐ GRAPHICS

PRODUCTION
RED DWARF VI
GUNMEN

PROJECT NO.

comprehend these mechanoids and genetically engineered life forms that keep popping up everywhere.

Stage G is nestled in the centre of Shepperton. An ancient red wooden door, still bearing the remnants of some old film poster, opens on to the *Red Dwarf* sets. Down one side of the stage are the sets which represent Starbug's interior. On the far left is the cockpit, which has been enlarged and modified for the present series. Connected to the cockpit is the mid-section, which features an airlock, monitors, the stairway and gantry leading to the upper level, and a green flat bed scanner surrounded by chairs. Right of that is the kitchen section or galley, and next to that is the ops room with its scanning computers and medi-bed. Behind this block of sets are the engine room and corridor section, which runs from the ops room to the mid-section, and is connected by several airlocks. Directly opposite the standing sets are the rows of audience seating, where nearly three hundred *Red Dwarf* fans show up every Saturday night for six weeks to watch the recording of their favourite programme. Next to the audience seating area a large space is reserved for any new sets which may be required. In one episode the area may be occupied by an elaborate dinning hall as in 'Legion', or even a thatched hut to match the 'Emohawk' medieval village exterior. It is in this space that the Last Chance Saloon will be built for 'Gunmen'.

At 8 a.m., set designer Mel Bibby, his assistant Steve Bradshaw, and the stagehands arrive at Stage G to dismantle Rimmer's Throne Room set, which was used in the previous recording. Mel joined the *Red Dwarf* team during season III, while the programme was still being recorded in Manchester, and wasted no time in making scenic improvements. Out went the cramped, claus-

Set designer Mel Bibby

trophobic sleeping quarters and dingy grey corridors that characterized the early years and, in their place, a new high-tech look started to take shape.

In *Red Dwarf VI*, much of which takes place in Starbug, there were six sets built to represent its interior: a modified cockpit, the mid-section, the galley, an ops room, the engine room, and a new corridor section. 'The big difference this year has been a two-tier situation,' says Mel. 'That was quite a challenge: to create a staircase, a gantry and everything else, and also get lights above it. Also the navicomps are new in the cockpit. They're actually part of a navigation system used for yachts. They're programmed with a map of the Greek islands, which look something like an asteroid belt. I think that's the best way to look at *Red Dwarf*: it's not an exact science. It's more suck it and see. That means if you can't find something, you have to

improvise. There are compromises that have to be made, especially when you have problems with budget, but *Red Dwarf* is a collective collaboration between a lot of departments, and whatever is needed eventually gets done.'

'Usually by me,' chips in Steve, with uncharacteristic bravado. Mel fixes him with a 'that'll cost you three pints of bitter later in the bar' look, and they go about their business.

By 9.30, the old set has been broken down, and lighting director John Pomphrey starts rigging his lights. In the late morning, the new sections for the saloon are delivered, and when John finishes, Mel, Steve and the stage crew move in to put it together.

By the end of the day, the Last Chance Saloon has been assembled, painted, and dressed with the necessary props and furniture. According to Steve, their set has been care-

fully designed to match the Laredo village exteriors, which will be shot on Tuesday. 'Originally, the western scenes were going to be shot in sepia, but we're not sure if they're still going to do that. Whether they stay with that idea or decide to keep the natural colour, you'll notice the saloon is painted in natural sepia-tones.'

Meanwhile, costume designer Howard Burden is putting together the extensive wardrobe for 'Gunmen'. Having spent part of the previous day hiring stock from the BBC, he is now meeting with a supplier in the West End, who will be providing most of the authentic western costumes for the principal characters. 'Our brief is that they should be as realistic as possible. With the added proviso, as with all *Red Dwarf* costumes, that they should be as close to free as possible. We don't have the funds to get a new set of cowboy duds made for each character, which would then have to be broken down and made more realistic. Instead, I'm using specialists who deal specifically with cowboy outfits, and I tell them each item of clothing I need for each character.'

MONDAY

At 10 a.m. the cast, director and writers gather around the flat bed scanner which doubles as a table in the mid-section of Starbug and 'Gunmen' is read out loud for the first time. There is much laughter, the mood is buoyant.

While director Andy DeEmmony begins to rehearse the physical moves – where the actors will sit, when they will rise etc. – Rob and Doug announce they'll be in their office 'trying to think of some more jokes'. Craig Charles shouts after them: 'Especially for me, guys, I've got none this week.' There is a roar of laughter from the rest of the cast –

this is a standing joke – Craig never believes he has any funny lines until he hears the audience reaction on show night.

As rehearsals proceed, several members of the production team make their way to the Laredo Western Club to set up for the following day's location filming. Mel and Steve arrive after lunch, armed with a lorry full of props and set dressing that will be used to alter and improve the existing store-fronts. The general store is turned into the Last Chance Saloon by replacing the sign in front and installing a pair of swinging, bat-wing doors. Another building down the block becomes the new general store, complete with outdoor shelves full of groceries, dry goods, pots and pans. The hitching post outside the store is replaced with a lightweight prop that will be used in Rimmer's fight with one of the Four Horsemen.

John Pomphrey begins setting up his lights, which will be vital in establishing the flow between location and studio scenes. 'I'm putting lamps with orange and straw-coloured gels inside each building to create a warm lighting effect. This in turn will create an environment for the studio stuff, which will also be done in warm tones. Basically, I decided how I would light the studio, and now I'm making the location look the same.'

Andy arrives in Laredo a few hours later, having pleaded with the cast 'to learn as much as they possibly could!' The director has story-boarded the key sequences, and he discusses those shots with the camera crew, working out where the crane and cameras will be positioned. He and Rocket, the show's permanently bobble-hatted camera supervisor, walk through each of the set-ups to anticipate any problems that might arise tomorrow.

As one of the founders of Telegenic, *Red Dwarf*'s OB

facilities, Rocket is the man responsible for capturing the director's vision on tape and making sure that the cameras are in place and ready to roll, both in the studio and on location. '*Red Dwarf* is shot in two guises,' Rocket explains. 'We shoot a lot of it as though it was a single-camera drama, because that's the only way to do the special effects, and get the performance level we need. At the same time, it's also done as a conventional TV show, which is multi-camera and a different discipline. This show is very visual, and it is very funny as well as being a dramatic piece. It's a style we could extend even further, given the chance. I think it's fairly common knowledge that I don't think we should shoot any of this in front of an audience. I'm all in favour of the audience seeing the show: watching scenes from it, and meeting the stars – seeing the reactions is a very important part of it – but the show itself and the way we tell stories has grown beyond the confines of doing it for two hours on a stage in front of a studio audience.'

Back at Shepperton, Howard's department is co-ordinating costume deliveries, getting their stock together, and loading up the wardrobe van. Each character's costume is hung on a rail with a bag of accessories, such as gun belts, hats and scarves, so when the artists come in the following morning everything will be ready for them.

A similar process is taking place in the make-up department, where Andria Pennell's team is loading up its supplies. Although most of the extras, who are members of the Laredo Western Club, reportedly have authentic period hairstyles, Andria packs plenty of spare beards, moustaches and sideburns, just in case.

TUESDAY

Filming starts early on the streets of the Laredo Western
Village, in order to take full advantage of existing daylight.
The make-up and costume trailers are in place by 5 a.m.
in a muddy field just outside the village gate. Robert
Llewellyn has the first make-up call, and the morning's
routine goes smoothly, until the other artists start to filter
in. The trailer has no stabilizers, and bounces badly every
time someone steps inside. For Andria and her assistant
Lois Burwell, who are working around Robert's eyes with
make-up brushes and glue, the process becomes a night-
mare. It's not a happy experience for the actor either.
'Whenever anyone came in or left, I got a glue brush up
my nose, or in my ear, or in my eye. I had to have a walk
in the field and kick a log afterwards to calm down.'

Andria Pennell and Lois Burwell explain step by step how Kryten's make-up is applied. 'We start by preparing the mask; painting and highlighting it, and trimming away any nasty bits of foam. A special prosthetic paint called PAX is used to seal the mask. Otherwise, it would absorb the make-up and turn a dirty colour.

'The actual make-up time is about two hours, although we could probably cut that down to one and three-quarters if seriously pushed for time. We start by gelling Robert's hair down, and heating up a bald cap with a hair-drier. The cap is placed over his head, the edges are trimmed, and the cap is fixed in place.

'Then we start with the mask. The piece is placed over Robert's head, we line everything up, place one hand on his forehead, and begin gluing it down. We work from the forehead downwards, starting with the forehead to the eyebrows, to the bridge of the nose, to the nose, to the top of the

A MECHANOID

lip, to the chin, and to the neck. Then we work out to the cheeks, doing the left one first.

'Next, it's time to get the seams together on the sides of the mask. Each of us takes one, so we're not pulling on it at the same time, which can distort the mask. Once the seams are glued together, you've got the complete mask. All that's left are the lips and eyes. We glue the bottom lip down, followed by the top, and each of us glues around one of the eyes. Once they're done, we seal around the lips with Duo surgical adhesive. We also seal around the eyes, using Pros-Aide instead of Duo, which contains ammonia.

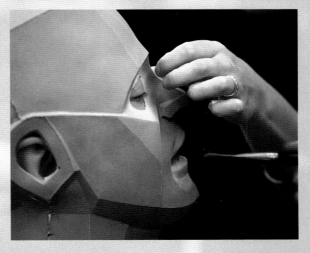

'Once the lips are dry, we can start to colour the lips and around the eyes, using a greaseless William Tuttle prosthetic base. At this point, we usually put in the mesh grates that cover Robert's ears. Then we have a cup of tea, finish the make-up using eye-liners and mascara, and, finally, we wave goodbye to Kryten.'

By 8.15 a.m., the artists have been through make-up and wardrobe, and start wandering on to the set. The Laredo Western Village is a stunningly realistic-looking location, and it's easy to see why Rob and Doug were impressed by it. One side of the street features the Town Marshal's Office, the Assay and Land Registry, and a lean-to that houses the local blacksmith. Each building is maintained by a different member of the club, who furnishes and continues to add to it. The Assay Office, for example, is run by a pair of very realistic cowboys named John and A.J., who invite members of the crew inside and offer them steaming cups of thick black coffee poured from an ancient kettle. Directly across the street from the Marshal's Office is the Last Chance Saloon, a two-storey building that advertises 'Cigarettes and Whisky and Wild, Wild Women'.

Craig steps out of the Assay Office, fortified by a cup of A.J.'s coffee. He's dressed in a black fringed jacket, gloves and hat, and his wide grin tells everyone how much fun he's having. He swaggers up to Chris Barrie, who is wearing a well-worn cowboy costume and long coat. The holo-gramatic 'H' on his forehead is almost obscured by a grey hat. He too is clearly enjoying himself. 'This would be a highlight in any performer's career,' Chris declares, 'getting to saddle up and fiddle around with guns in a western town. Just being able to don these outfits is a great experience.'

Craig agrees: 'It's a fantasy come true. How often do you get to be a cowboy for a day?'

Robert Llewellyn is standing a few feet away, dressed in a dingy western outfit, and looking terribly out of place in his rubbery Kryten mask. He's wearing a heavy blue ski-jacket over his shoulders to protect himself from the early morning chill, and still seems to be suffering from his earlier painful experience in the make-up trailer. He brightens up when Craig holds a gun to his own temple and recreates the classic 'Don't move, or the nigger gets it' scene from *Blazing Saddles*.

Danny John Jules rides up on his horse, provoking a roar of laughter from the crew. Danny is dressed in a black and silver matador costume, similar to the outfits worn in the Steve Martin/Chevy Chase film *The Three Amigos*. As Danny recalled later: 'That was my favourite memory – the look on everybody's faces when I first rode into town as the Riviera Kid. People couldn't believe it, and the biggest smiles belonged to Rob and Doug. They were red-faced bursting with laughter – I wish I'd had a camera.'

It's a beautiful, sunny day, and the sense of relief from director and producers is almost tangible. A few minutes of rain could easily have turned the dirt road running through the centre of town back into a massive mud slick.

The scenes are not filmed in script order. The production team decide on a shooting order based on getting the most footage with the least set-ups and camera repositioning. As logic would have it, the first scene of the day is a scene from the middle of the sequence: a confrontation

between Kryten and the Four Horsemen, which takes place in front of the saloon.

EXT.   STREETS OF LAREDO   DAY
The FOUR HORSEMEN OF THE APOCALYPSE *sit menacingly on horseback outside the saloon. The bat-wing doors part and a nervous* KRYTEN *emerges swigging from a bottle of hooch.*

KRYTEN:
I don't believe I've had the pleasure, sirs.

DEATH *spits out some chewing-tobacco, which fizzles on the street like acid.*

DEATH:
The name's Death. And these here're my brothers. Brother War . . .

WAR *laughs and flames shoot out of his mouth.*

DEATH:
Brother Famine . . .

Fat FAMINE *nods and takes a bit of chicken.*

DEATH:
and Brother Pestilence.

PESTILENCE *grins, showing horrible broken teeth. He swipes idly at the swarm of buzzing flies around his head.*

KRYTEN:
Well, you seem like a nice neighbourly bunch of boys. How can I be of service?

All FOUR APOCALYPSE BOYS *draw, shooting* KRYTEN*'s hat off, and his bottle out of his hand, as he dances around trying to avoid the hail of bullets. Finally the gunfire stops.*

DEATH:
We want your sorry ass out of here. You got one hour.

DEATH *spits a sizzler again, and* THE FOUR HORSEMEN *turn and gallop under a dangling sign: 'YOU ARE NOW LEAVING EXISTENCE', and as the* HORSEMEN *ride under it, they disappear.* KRYTEN *takes off his sheriff's star and throws it on the floor.*

Simon Wallace, the first assistant, positions the Four Horsemen in front of the saloon. Robert is called in, and after removing his ski-jacket, he takes his position on the steps. In the blink of an eye, he shifts into his drunken sheriff persona, stumbling and staggering back and forth.

The cameras roll, as Kryten, whisky bottle in one hand, is taunted by the Four Horsemen. As they start shooting, a compressed air gun off-camera fires pellets of coloured powder, making it appear as if bullets are hitting the ground. The combination of loud noise and compressed air proves to be too much for the horses. One of them rears and throws stunt man Robert (War) Inch, while Denis (Death) Lill's mount bolts, and he has to circle a nearby field several times before his horse has calmed down. After giving War and Death a few minutes to recover, the scene is replayed successfully. Each of the Four Horsemen is then repositioned for individual close-ups.

The next shot has War shooting fire from his mouth. Robert Inch takes a large gulp of paraffin from a disposable cup and holds it in his mouth. The director calls for action, and Inch brandishes a torch, igniting an impressive stream of flame. 'I learned fire breathing working at a theme park,' he explains. 'There was a resident fireblower, and I picked up the trade from him. The stunts we're doing today are quite dangerous, especially because we're outside. You never know what the wind is going to do, and being on horseback makes it even more difficult, because you have to anticipate what the horse is going to do at the same time.'

'No wonder,' offers Robert Llewellyn, 'he turned down the baked beans at breakfast.'

As Andy re-shoots the sequence several times to get a better view of the flames, the other cast members mix with some of the 'locals'. Although numerous film and TV crews have visited Laredo in the past, the club members are still tremendously excited to be meeting the *Red Dwarf* posse. Cameras magically appear, and throughout the day scenes of cast and cowboys posing together are commonplace.

EXT.   STREETS OF LAREDO   DAY

The APOCALYPSE BOYS *walk slowly through the swirling mist and stop at the far end of the street.* KRYTEN *steps out of the Sheriff's Office followed by* LISTER, RIMMER *and* CAT. *They fan out across the street.*

Director Andy DeEmmony positions the boys for their big showdown

By late morning, the sun has moved to a favourable position, and the crew prepares for a new set-up in front of the livery stables at the end of the block. Howard Burden dusts Robert's coat down with Fuller's Earth to give it a dirtier look, then hands it back to the actor.

Danny is standing on the steps of the nearby Registry Office, practising his Riviera Kid dance; an exaggerated Flamenco step with a touch of Mexican hat dance thrown in for good measure. 'It's nice to do something different. By playing the Riviera Kid, I'm getting to widen the scope of my character. Those stories, like "Gunmen", which tend to stretch you a bit more are always a good experience.'

Simon calls for positions. They're ready to shoot the story's climactic scene, where the boys confront the Four Horsemen. What the *Dwarf* posse don't know is that the virus has spread to the Artificial Reality Console, cancelling out their special abilities. Craig, Chris, Robert and Danny take their places in the saloon while the Four Horsemen wait for their cue inside the stables a few yards away.

Peter Wragg's visual effects team fills the area with smoke from several portable smoke machines. The cameras roll, and the Four Horsemen emerge from the swirling mist. On a second 'action!', Robert steps out of the saloon, followed by his three companions.

'Got yourself a little help, Sheriff?' asks Denis, stepping forward. He smiles grimly as Kryten recognizes him as a manifestation of the computer virus. 'Have infection will travel, that's me. Now, let's see if we can't tip the balance a little here . . .' He raises his hands skywards, where a flash of lightning will be added in post-production.

Chris Barrie approaches the Four Horsemen, and Denis signals the actor playing War to meet his challenge. War

strides over to the prop hitching post outside the general store, belches fire on it, and tears off a smoking chunk of wood. Brandishing the club, he begins beating Chris over the head with it. The crew laugh, as Chris does a convincing stagger and near-fall. It genuinely appears as if he's been hit with a heavy piece of wood.

Two buildings away, Andy, Rob and Doug watch the take on a monitor set up in the shelter of the blacksmith's stall. A single shot follows of Chris and Robert Inch, as Rimmer realizes his fist-fighting abilities have vanished, leaving him powerless. He begins clapping his hands together, trying to activate the glove control that will return him to reality, but nothing happens. Chris starts an exaggerated tap dance, clapping his hands, and circling a confused War who has no idea what is going on. 'Not funny!' says Doug, after watching the shot. 'All the comedy is in the feet,' he explains to Andy, who has been shooting Chris from the waist up, effectively losing much of the comedic effect. The director doesn't quite agree with the inherent humour of Chris's jig, but agrees to a wider shot. In the end, the writer's suggestion does look funnier.

For the next few hours, scenes of the crew escaping the Artificial Reality game are filmed in rapid succession. In order to take maximum advantage of the existing sunlight, the crew goes to lunch in shifts, making their way to the muddy field outside the village where the catering van has been parked. Because it's such a beautiful day, most of the extras decide to eat their lunch outdoors, and the sight of a few dozen cowboys standing in a pasture, their plates piled high with chicken curry, topped with popadoms, is a strange one indeed.

Meanwhile, Robert Llewellyn is being prepared for the final confrontation between Sheriff Kryten and the Four

Horsemen. Inside the saloon, Peter Wragg and his assistants wire the actor up with a series of small explosive charges, which will be triggered from a control box. They also glue a pair of hand-carved dove attachments, sculpted by Paul McGuiness, to Robert's guns.

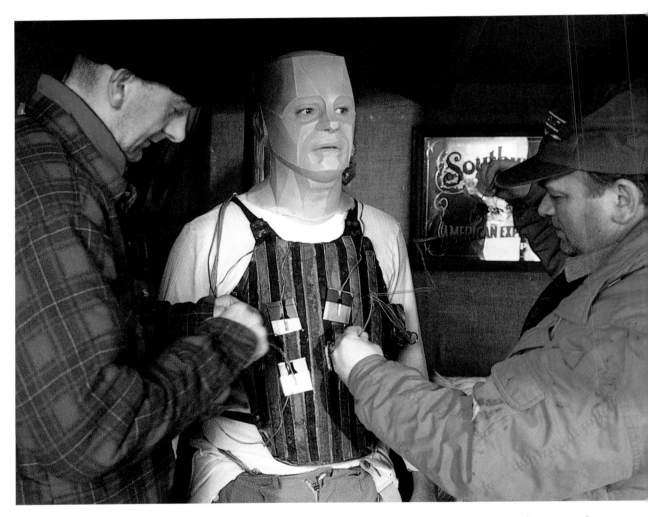

The visual effects team wires up Robert Llewellyn for his explosive confrontation with the Four Horsemen

With Robert now wired up, he returns to the set, where the props department has a cage full of doves standing by. As the cameras roll, Peter Wragg triggers his charges, creating the illusion of Kryten being riddled by the Horsemen's bullets. Robert staggers back, pulls his pistols, and then drops them on the ground.

'Don't move a muscle!' shouts Andy. The doves are brought in and placed in Robert's hands, and the director calls for action. Sheriff Kryten pulls out the doves as if they're being drawn from his holsters, and lets the birds fly – or tries to, anyway. The doves' wings have been clipped, so they can't fly. As Robert releases them they flutter up to about a foot and then fall to the ground. A second take produces the same results, and on the third try an exasperated Andy tells Robert, 'Once more. And give them a real lob this time!' The third try isn't much better, and ultimately the scene will have to be remounted in another location, with doves that fly.

EXT.   STREETS OF LAREDO   DAY

CAT *does the Riviera Kid dance, draws his gun, and fires behind his back. The bullet hits a tin bath and ricochets across the street, where it hits a bell and ricochets again. Wide shot of street as the bullet zig-zags towards* KRYTEN, *finally severing the support on one side of the dangling 'EXISTENCE' sign, which swings down and flattens* KRYTEN.

It is almost 4 p.m., and the crew set up for a shot where the Cat shoots the 'YOU ARE NOW LEAVING EXISTENCE' sign, which falls on Kryten's head. The realistic-looking foam sign has been rigged by the effects team to fall on cue, and Andy calls for action. In a single, continuous shot, Robert bursts out of the saloon, runs down the street and under the sign. With split second timing, the sign drops squarely on his head, and Robert does a spectacular pratfall, worthy of Buster Keaton. The take is absolutely perfect, and the entire crew applauds. Andy checks the playback on his monitor, gives a thumbs up, and Sheriff Kryten goes off to have some minor repair work done on his head. 'That was a fluke!' the actor admits. 'We hadn't tried that before, nothing had been tested, but somehow it worked. That was a once-a-series occurrence!'

EXT.   STREETS OF LAREDO   DAY

SLO-MO:
*The GUNMEN draw and fire. Four shots slam into
KRYTEN's chest. He staggers, then straightens, and
draws both his guns.*
*As the guns leave his holster they both transform
into white doves, which soar off into the sky.*
The GUNMEN collapse and slowly fade away.

At 5 p.m., one of the crew members announces they are
rapidly losing sunlight. With only a limited amount of time
available, Andy begins to pick up the pace. The crew
returns to the saloon for a quick shot of Death spitting
acidic chewing-tobacco on Kryten's boot. For the close-
ups, Peter Wragg uses a bottle of TTC, a caustic substance

that produces impressive wisps of white smoke. 'It's very unpleasant,' warns Peter. 'We can only use it outside.' After several takes Andy finds one he is happy with.

EXT.   STREETS OF LAREDO   DAY

Through a swirling mist LISTER, CAT *and* RIMMER *gallop into town.*

'We're only just going to make it ... just,' declares John Pomphrey. 'The sun is dipping down very quickly!' With only 15 or 20 minutes of usable daylight left, Craig, Chris and Danny still have their horseback scene to shoot. 'I want all the extras up at this end,' Andy announces, and a dozen of the locals take their places along the street near the stables. 'Cue horses!' the director calls, and the cowboys from the Dwarf ride into town, stopping in front of the saloon. They dismount, and enter the building, as the crew watches intently. This scene will have to be blended seamlessly with an interior shot of the boys entering the saloon to be shot on Thursday.

The final sequence of the day is a special shot requested by Rob and Doug of the four Dwarfers galloping into town on horseback, which hopefully will be used in the opening credits montage for this series. Rocket's crane is raised high in the air, and Andy calls for action. The boys gallop into town, past the cameras, and down the street in one impressive take. 'Oh lovely!' declares Andy, watching the shot on the monitor. Simon calls a wrap, and John Pomphrey reaches up and strikes an ancient triangular dinner bell hanging from one of the storefronts. The crew starts the long process of de-rigging and packing up the equipment for the long drive back to Shepperton.

WEDNESDAY

Each of the departments is in the studio early, to begin unloading and unpacking the vans. The costumes have been piled in a large heap in the wardrobe department, and Howard's staff has to sort through them, making sure the clothing and accessories for each artist are there.

Rehearsals start at 11 a.m. with the four principals and a few guest artists, including Steve Devereaux who will play Jimmy, and Imogen Bain as Lola the bartender. There is still a feeling of euphoria among the cast and crew after yesterday's successful filming day in Laredo. According to Andy, much of that success is due to advance planning. 'I had to know all the scenes we were doing, where the cameras had to be positioned, and where the crane would be. With the crane, I was able to cover various shots

without moving, but we were also shooting out of sequence with shots all over the place, which is very difficult for the cast. The very hard bit was maintaining the energy so everything flowed, but in the end I think we did. Basically, I had all the story-boards which I had finished the night before, and as we struggled through the day I was able to tick the frames off, so I had all the shots we needed to connect.'

Andy is particularly happy with their use of a crane, which resulted in some amazing shots. 'Rob and Doug didn't want to use it, because they felt elaborate establishing shots were always the first thing to be cut in the edit, where you're always trying to give the comedy a good pacey feel, but we talked them into taking a crane up to Laredo, and by getting through the rest of it, we had time to do that big opening shot, which I think sets it up beautifully. It was nice to open it up and get that feeling of space.'

Rocket, *Red Dwarf*'s long-suffering camera supervisor

Also pleased with yesterday's work is Rocket, the camera supervisor, who has shot some very complicated sequences during his years on *Red Dwarf*. 'I didn't think we'd get the Laredo footage in the time we had allotted, at the level we did,' he admits. 'In fact, my advice was we should have been in the village for two days. Without a doubt, the biggest risk, and the most difficult thing we took on, was to shoot that script in the time we did but, touch wood, it was successful.'

Robert Llewellyn remembered: 'When we were all on horses for the ride past the cameras at the end of the day, I found that scene very funny, because it distilled the essence of our four characters, if you like. I've ridden horses a lot, and I've also fallen off them a lot, so I have plenty of experience with that, and therefore fear. Chris

'This is a job for the Riviera Kid!'

STORY-BOARDS

Since each episode of *Red Dwarf* is shot out of sequence, director Andy DeEmmony created story-boards (a series of panels, with rough drawings depicting changes of scene or action) for the major sequences. By checking off each scene as it was shot, Andy would have all the necessary footage at the end of the day.

On the pages following are Andy DeEmmony's story-boards from 'Gunmen', used on location in Laredo, as well as the stage directions taken from the actual script. By comparing them to still frames from the finished episode, it is possible to see how the director ultimately interprets a script.

STREET OF LAREDO   DAY

1. CAT *does riviera dance, draws his gun, aims his gun to the side and fires behind his back. The bullet hits a tin bath and ricochets across the street, where it hits a bell and ricochets again ...*

2. *...* wide shot of street as the bullet zigzags towards KRYTEN, *finally severing the support on one side of the dangling 'existence' sign, which swings down and flattens* KRYTEN.

3. *The* APOCALYPSE BOYS *walk slowly through the swirling mist and stop ...*

4. *...* KRYTEN *steps out to face them.*

5. ALL FOUR *Apocalypse Boys draw ...*

6. *... shoot* KRYTEN*'s hat off, his bottle out of his hand, and he dances around trying to avoid the hail of bullets.*

hasn't ridden a lot, but is a sensible human being, and therefore was also scared. Danny has ridden a bit, and is actually very good, so he wasn't scared. Craig had never ridden a horse before in his life, but he has no fear, and therefore was extremely dangerous. He kept saying "giddi-up!" and those horses were very frisky. They were also capable of attaining incredible speeds, as I soon discovered. It was a funny day.'

The rehearsals continue until 4 p.m., followed by the 'Tech Run', in which the director, cast, writers, producer, department heads and technical staff watch an uncostumed run-through of the parts of the script that will be shot tomorrow and Friday. Rocket acts as a dummy camera, contorting into curious poses, holding his hands to his eyes to 'frame' the shots, checking to see if the angles will work, and whether a special camera may be needed where a studio pedestal can't get in close enough for a shot.

After the Tech Run, the cast go home to study their lines, and the production team gets together for the weekly planning meeting. Tonight, they're going over the script for 'Emohawk', the next episode to be filmed. Each department head offers his or her input, discussing how various effects can be handled, and how new characters such as the GELFs will be created, and by whom.

Steve Wickham, as an overly amorous GELF in 'Emohawk'

THURSDAY

The pre-VT day is probably the most difficult part of the week for the cast and crew; starting at 10 a.m. and running up until 10 p.m., and sometimes even later. The pre-VT filming is devoted to scenes which are too complex to be recorded live before the studio audience. Scenes that require special effects, split screens, explosions, or fight sequences. The scenes that will be shot today will then be edited overnight and played to the audience on the studio TV, thus allowing their laughter to be recorded as if live.

Today's schedule is especially demanding. The saloon scene, which will take most of the day to record, involves more than a dozen extras, a trick bullwhip, a knife-throwing sequence, a gunfight, and a knock-down, drag-out fight between Chris Barrie and several stunt men.

The morning is very difficult for Howard Burden's costume department, who have to deal with a new batch of characters. 'We have principals like Lola, and Jimmy the card shark, whose costumes have complications,' says Howard. 'With Jimmy, the knives are going to go through his shirt, so I have to have doubles ready, and I also had to have bits and pieces for some of the other characters like Bear Strangler McGee. Originally, Rimmer was supposed to vomit in his hat, but now they've decided they're going to mime it, so we don't need the vomitless double.

INT.   SALOON   DAY

Busy. A PIANO PLAYER *plays a honky tonk version of* Red Dwarf *theme:* KRYTEN *enters and tries to steer his way towards the bar. He passes* JIMMY – *a smooth oaf, playing cards with some unruly* COWPOKES – *who trips him up.*

By 10.15, Andy is ready to rehearse the first scene. The saloon is filled with extras, dressed in western clothing, and seated at various tables, or leaning against the wall. The set looks impressive, painted in soft, earthy tones, dressed with authentic looking props, such as bull horns, oil lamps and animal skulls, and beautifully lit by John Pomphrey. A large window near the door allows in light from the 'outside', and John has adjusted his lamps to match yesterday's bright sunlight.

If there is one man who has helped to maintain the visual continuity of *Red Dwarf* over its six-year history, it is lighting director John Pomphrey. John's colourful, evocative lighting has been a fixture of the programme since the very first episode. In order to create a distinctive style for the show, John was actually influenced by his work in another genre. 'When I wasn't doing *Red Dwarf*, I was doing rock and pop shows, so I was heavily into the music colours and I carried that over. My musical tastes run to heavy metal and I would go to concerts and see groups like Iron Maiden and outrageous bands like that, and in a way they had a similar style. If you look at them they're into the same colours I am: oranges, deep blues; powerful colours. I don't believe in understating something, because you're generally watching it on a small screen in a well-lit room, so you've got to overstate the colours. In the cinema, you can get away with subtle tones, but I don't think you can on this show. When they write it, Rob and Doug have in their mind's eye exactly how they want it to look. I've got to get on their wavelength, the same as the director. Before this series I had never met Andy. He's a bit of a photographer, so he knows pictures and has a good visual eye. He told me he likes light and shade, and lots of dark corners, and he wanted *Red Dwarf* to have even more of a filmic look. In the end that's fine with me because I'm a frustrated cinematographer: I want to make *Aliens*.'

Even after six years of *Red Dwarf*, John still finds the programme exciting to work on and his job is not without its hazards as he discovered during the location filming on 'Terrorform' last year. 'It was autumn, and we were filming near this river,' he ruefully recalls. 'There was a lot of grass

John Pomphrey, the programme's colourful lighting director

around and the banks were completely overgrown, and our electrician fell in. I stepped forward to help him out, offered him my hand, stepped on what I thought was grass and went straight in too. The morale of the crew skyrocketed, because it was seven at night, it had just got dark, and we were supposed to be shooting until four in the morning. There I was, lying there next to the electrician, my pockets filled with water – it was a great loss to my dignity. Since then I have been constantly baited about the incident, and when the crew turned up this year on the same location, there was a life-jacket hanging on the side of the lighting truck, especially for me!'

The next scene is a quick reaction shot of Jimmy holding out his pistol, and then holstering it. The sequence will later be played backwards, as if the cowboy's arm is being pinned to the wall by a knife. It's a difficult scene to

Vis-fx assistant James Davis runs through the knife-throwing sequence with Andy DeEmmony

choreograph and Andy runs through the action over and over until it starts to look realistic.

Near by, Robert is relaxing in Starbug's mid-section. Between the mask, the heavy costume and the hot studio lights, Thursday is probably the most uncomfortable day for him, and in between scenes he tries to exert himself as little as possible. 'It's very difficult,' he explains. 'My eyes get extremely tired, and I don't really know why that happens. I think it's the combination of the mask being very hot, and the only place I can lose the heat from my head is through the skin around my eyes. Normally, when the light shines in your eyes, you unconsciously do something to shield yourself from it, but when I have got this mask on, it affects my vision so that I don't know where the bloody lights are coming from, and it really hurts. Fortunately, the physical side effects are at a minimum this year. They're really very, very low, so that's a bit of a relief.'

The music that will accompany today's scene has already been pre-recorded by composer Howard Goodall, who normally does most of his work for the series after the final episode has been recorded. 'With "Gunmen", we obviously wanted a score that would be some sort of western pastiche. I composed an epic going-off-into-the-sunset type thing and at the end of the episode the western theme we developed throughout the programme takes over the final credits, turning into the *Red Dwarf* theme half-way through. Doing a western's been great. But that's the fun of the show – the concepts they come up with are amazing and whenever a new series comes along, you always think, "What are they going to come up with this time?" '

Craig walks on to the set in his now-familiar cowboy outfit, followed by Danny, and Chris who has been in the corridor for the past half-hour with stunt co-ordinator Gerard Naprous, rehearsing his upcoming fight scene. Danny is even more excited than usual. He's come up with a new line that he wants Rob and Doug to put in the script. 'I've come for the man who shot my paw!' he announces in his best Clint Eastwood voice. 'How much do you want to bet I get that line in today?' Nobody takes the bet. It's a pity. They would have made money.

INT.   SALOON   DAY

RIMMER *downs the whisky, gulping. The smile freezes on his face. He grabs the hat from a near-by* COWPOKE, *and is sick into it. Music and talk stop. The* COWPOKE *stands and looms, making* RIMMER *look shorter than a Clint Eastwood speech. Chairs scrape back from tables.*

Rimmer meets Bear Strangler
McGee (Stephen Marcus)

The cowpoke character, played by Stephen Marcus, is absolutely enormous, and as he stands up, a massive shadow is thrown over Chris. Instead of adjusting his lighting to compensate for the shadow, John Pomphrey suggests leaving it in, making the scene even funnier.

Most of the crew break for a well-deserved lunch, although as always, there are a few people who stay behind. One of them is editor Graham Hutchings, who spends most of the day in the scanner, satisfying himself that all the footage will cut together. During the break in the recording, Graham explains how an episode of *Red Dwarf* is edited. 'My work starts well before the final recording day,' he begins, 'when I start looking at the scripts with Rob, Doug and the director to get a clear idea of what might affect the final product in terms of editing. We go through the scripts, decide what can and can't be done, and if there's anything particularly difficult, we consult the effects people, and try and work our way around it.

'The next stage begins the Monday after the studio, when I do a rough assemble of the show to get everything in story order, and cut together all the preferred takes we've marked up on the studio nights. This gives us an idea if everything has worked and a chance to see if there are any flaws in the footage or if we need to do any re-shoots. After looking at all the rushes and rough assemblies, Andy and I will rough-cut the show, and, having looked at it, there may be other problems that have arisen. We may have to re-brief the video effects people, or even Peter Wragg, if it means changing shots to make them work.

'Our next step is to get the notes from Rob and Doug and do a fine cut, to reduce the running time. Coming out of the studio, most episodes generally run nine to ten minutes over length but we can cut most of that down simply by tightening the performances. Virtually no breath of dialogue is left untouched, although we try and protect all the laughs we can. At this point, the video effects are still being processed, so we have to imagine what they will look like. We give them a tape with the programme cuts, on to which they "paint" the effects. Finally, after the last on-line edit, when we've got it to length, and the effects are all cut in, the episodes go to the BBC to be dubbed. Sound effects, atmosphere and music are added over a four day period, and then it comes back to me for the final credits and opening titles, which we do last because they incorporate shots from all the different episodes.

'I would say *Red Dwarf* is undoubtedly the best pro-gramme I work on during the year. I love the way Rob and Doug write, and there's nothing on British television that comes anywhere near it. When you get to the end of the editing process and look at these episodes you think, "My God, these are startling pieces of work!" Creatively that's the greatest feeling you could have.'

When the crew return from lunch, Andy starts rehears-ing some of the more difficult action that has to be shot, including the bullwhip and knife sequences. For a scene

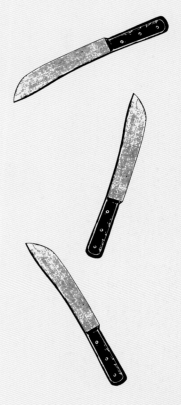

In the post-*Terminator II* world of special effects, the producers of *Red Dwarf* have continued experimenting with cutting-edge technology to maintain the show's outstanding visuals. With *Red Dwarf VI*, that process takes a leap forward, thanks to the work of SVC Television's Terry Hylton and Karl Mooney. The London based facilities house has supplied an astonishing range of electronic effects, from laser blasts and gunshots to elaborate morphing effects and 3D animation. SVC's principal tool is Quantel's HARRY, a graphics-orientated machine with almost unlimited potential. According to Terry, 'It allows you to process, manipulate, composite, retouch and recolour live action footage on a frame by frame basis. You can build up levels of elements shot against blue screen, and it's all digital, so whatever you do stays at first class quality.'

'Gunmen' required a wide range of effects, from a computer virus, to the cloud of flies surrounding Pestilence. 'With the virus, I wanted to show Kryten affected on the outside,' Karl recalls, 'but Rob and Doug thought it was important that it looked as if it entered him. In the end, I did a few shots of the virus entering Kryten, by using an

organic wipe. I put the same virus into the cowboys at the end of the episode.

'The flies were done in 3D. We used a particle system, with five little circles run through 3D. It's a very quick shot; only about 25 frames. We thought we might have to do some traditional animation, but the guys in 3D managed to come up with something quite convincing. I also did the graphics for the two computer games, and a lot of little flashes and gunshots. We devised a small morph for the scene when Kryten pulls out his hand-guns, which turn into doves, and added a paint effects frame and some lighting to a shot of Death pointing his arms in the air. There were a lot of bits for that episode.'

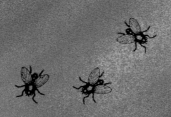

in which the whip is used to yank a bottle out of Kryten's hands, and a second sequence where the whip is cut in half by Lister's knife, two prop whips have been built by visual effects assistant Jim Davis: one already attached to a bottle, and another that will snap on cue.

The knife sequence is more difficult. To create the illusion of Jimmy's jacket being pinned to the saloon wall by Lister's knives, the actor, Steve Devereaux, is positioned against the wall, and a prop knife affixed to his sleeve. A thin nylon line is attached to the handle, and visual effects assistant Paul McGuiness stands on a chair, holding the line taut. On the director's cue, he yanks it back, and the knife flies out of the wall. By playing the scene in reverse at high speed, it will appear that the knives land bang on target.

With those scenes completed, the artists are called back to the set for live action elements. Robert starts complaining loudly to anyone who will listen, about having to stand next to Craig while he is throwing knives. His fears prove to be well founded. In the next scene, Lister is supposed to stab his knife into an apple, and flip it across the room, where it lodges in Jimmy's mouth. Unfortunately, to Craig's annoyance and the crew's amusement, the knife sticks to the apple like glue and it takes several attempts before the stubborn piece of fruit finally decides to co-operate.

INT.   SALOON   DAY

FRANK *and* NUKE *both draw and fire off a shot each. Back to the* CAT, *who casually draws and fires. There are two mid-air flashes half-way between the* CAT *and the* GUN-FIGHTERS, *and two bullets clatter to the floor.*

THE UNSEEN GUNMEN: LISTER TEACHES NUKE A LESSON

One of the scenes cut from the final script is an encounter between Lister and Nuke, one of Jimmy's henchmen. Although the sequence was never shot, it is still worth reading. 'I'm sorry that scene was cut,' notes Craig Charles, who had been looking forward to the stunt. 'I think it would have worked quite well!'

JIMMY:
Nail him, Nuke.

The piano stops, talking stops, chairs scrape. NUKE, one of Jimmy's larger cronies – unruly beard and hair – steps forward. LISTER, his back to Nuke, hears the gun being clicked.

LISTER:
[TO LOLA] You got any soapy water?

LOLA:
Got the stuff I clean the glasses in.

LISTER:
That'll do.

LISTER takes the wooden bucket of suds, turns and throws it over NUKE, covering his head with soap suds. LISTER throws a series of knives in rapid succession. We cut back to NUKE, who is now clean-shaven with slicked back hair with a centre parting.

LOLA:
Nice knife work.

LISTER:
Not so good. The sideburns are uneven.

'We're going to be firing a gun in this scene!' warns Simon. Justin blanches, and pretends he has to go off to make an important telephone call. In this scene, which will be partially enhanced in post-production, the Riviera Kid draws his guns and shoots the cowboys' bullets out of the air. In reality, the two stunt men are lightning fast and they draw their guns before Danny has a chance to react. He laughs: 'I may be the Kid, but I ain't that fast!' He recalled later: 'They were really fast on the draw, and I couldn't help thinking if this was a real gun situation I would have been shot in the head. In fact, those blanks peppered my face from across the room. I thought I'd really been shot.'

At 5.30 Denis Lill, who only two days earlier had been playing Death, walks on to the set, dressed as the Simulant Captain. According to today's running order, the crew should already be filming the Simulant scenes, but the

Denis Lill, the hard-working Simulant Captain

saloon effects have taken much longer than expected. With his black leather jacket, bushy moustache and a set of double eyebrows, Denis looks like a cross between a high-tech biker, Groucho Marx and a munchkin from *The Wizard of Oz*. 'Since Denis was supposed to be a Simulant, we wanted him to have a waxy look,' explains Andria, who designed the make-up. 'We put quite a thick base on him, and then let it go shiny. That gave him a strange plasticized appearance.'

The last scene before the dinner break is Rimmer's saloon fight with the four cowboys. Having practised off and on all day, Chris is ready to shine. As the cameras roll, he ducks under a chair being raised over his head, and punches the cowboy, knocking him down. He kicks a second cowboy into the wall, backhands a third into a table, and throws the fourth one over the bar. The cowboy

lands to the impressive sound of breaking glass. Chris Barrie's impression: 'We spent a goodly amount of time getting the fight scene in the saloon to look right. I kept thinking of different things to do, and thanks to Gerard and his stunt men we worked at it long and hard. I'll be watching that scene more than anything else in post-production, to see what's been done to it.'

Andy orders another take, the saloon is tidied up, and the extras return to their marks. The fight is re-staged a second time, then a third, until Andy is finally satisfied. He's not entirely happy with any one take, but by cutting back and forth between the three shots, he has enough footage to make it work.

After dinner, the cast and crew reassemble in the saloon for the final western sequences. While Lister tries to sober up Kryten with heaped spoonfuls of raw coffee (actually powdered chocolate, but the scene will still elicit groans when shown to the audience on Saturday), vision supervisor Mike Spencer is in the scanner, experimenting with the colour of the picture, which suddenly changes to sepia. Combined with the earthy tones of the saloon set, and John Pomphrey's skilful lighting, the scene playing on the monitors takes on the appearance of a 19th century antique photograph.

With the last saloon shot finished, the cast return to their dressing-rooms to change into their *Red Dwarf* costumes. The crew starts lighting the Simulant ship, which is barely recognizable as an escape pod used in 'Rimmerworld'. With blue, atmospheric lighting and strategically placed camera angles, the tiny set appears much larger on camera than it actually is. 'This was really designed for a one-off script,' explains Mel, who is busy adding bits of set decoration to the Simulant ship. 'We had to have a seat for Rimmer, who stands up and fires a flare, and that was it. Then the script for "Gunmen" came in which included a Simulant ship, so we looked at the escape pod and thought we could use it for this script as well. I think they look a bit too similar, but you can argue that they both came from the same ship, so it's not too bad. I might have been happier if we had sprayed it a different colour for this episode.'

As Liz and Denis take their places in the Simulant ship, the cast members start returning. Craig walks in carrying his boots, followed by Robert without the chest plate of his costume. They sit down at the table in Starbug's mid-section waiting for their next scene, along with Rocket and two of his cameramen. Chris joins the group, dressed in Rimmer's blue hard-light suit, and starts entertaining everyone with his letter-perfect impressions of the cast and crew. His imitation of Simon the floor manager is a particular favourite – so much so that by the end of the series, the entire cast are doing their own Simon Wallace impressions – and his impersonation of Justin Judd's low-slung trousers has been known to reduce members of the crew to tears of hysteria.

INT.   SIMULANT SHIP   DARK

The monitor comes to life. What appears to be a strange alien life form comes on screen. It is, in fact, the bottom half of LISTER*'s face, shot upside down below the nose. Taped to his chin are two antennae made out of pipe cleaners, with Kryten's spare eyes glued to the end.*

LISTER:
I am Tarka Dall, an ambassador of the great Vindalooian empire.

MODEL EFFECTS

With every series of *Red Dwarf*, Peter Wragg and his team of visual effects wizards manage to create a staggering array of high-quality model shots, with a budget that would make any Hollywood effects house wince with embarrassment.

In *Red Dwarf VI*, the model shots have reached a new level of richness and sophistication. Scenes of a blazing Starbug hurtling towards a smoking lava planet, a space battle, and an exploding Simulant battle cruiser were some of the scenes created for 'Gunmen'.

The large scale battle cruiser model, designed by Alan Marshall, was inspired by the western and science fiction elements contained in Rob and Doug's script. 'Initially, I had the idea of a skull-shaped spaceship to represent Death,' Alan recalls. 'Then, to make it a bit more evil, I thought a goat skull would make a better shape, with the main gun turrets on the end of the horns. Rob liked the idea of the skull, but suggested to fit it with the wild west feel of the episode, it should be the kind of skull you find in the deserts of Arizona. I made some adjustments, and the result is a ship that looks more like a cow skull; chunkier, less streamlined, with thicker more forceful horns.'

The battle cruiser's destruction was filmed using an ultra high-speed Photosonic camera. First, a series of explosions were rigged on the model's surface, followed by a larger blast that blew off one of the gun turret horns. For the final take, the effects team laced the ship with high explosives, and blew it into thousands of tiny fragments.

The climactic scene of 'Gunmen' saw Starbug plunging

The full-scale Simulant battle cruiser, built by Alan Marshal

into the surface of a bubbling lava planet. According to Peter Wragg, 'It was supposed to be crashing into water, but it's very difficult to make water look convincing in model shots. We persuaded Rob and Doug to let us do something else, so we created a lava planet for that episode.' For the lava sequence, Peter's team constructed an elaborate table-top miniature, consisting of a background mountain range, and Perspex tables filled with gelatinous goo, and underlit with oranges, reds and yellows. The surface was sprinkled with pieces of cork, rubber dust and charcoal, creating the illusion of lava, and a backdrop of a brooding orange, sulphurous sky completed the illusion. A slot was concealed in the set, and the Starbug model flew down at a 45 degree angle, triggering a burst of flames as it entered the slot.

Another shot was filmed, with a flaming Starbug emerging from the lava, as well as establishing shots of the planet's surface. These were ultimately cut together with shots of Starbug approaching a red glowing planet, a sunset element filmed by effects cameraman Peter Tyler, and live action elements of the crew shouting 'Yee-Hah!' inside the cockpit.

Peter Wragg's award-winning visual effects team prepare an elaborate model shot featuring Starbug

It's 9.45 p.m. and with only 15 minutes left in the scheduled recording day, Andy decides to try squeezing in the final shot: the Simulant Captain materializing on Starbug, where he finds Lister and Cat pretending to be aliens. Leaning backwards in their chairs, so the faces are upside down to the camera, neither crew member is aware of the Simulant Captain, who has materialized a few feet away.

Andy tries several takes, but it's very late in the day, and the cast members are having trouble with their lines. The scene is shelved until Saturday, and Simon calls it a wrap.

FRIDAY

Andy and the cast come in to rehearse Saturday's scenes; doing word runs and speed runs to make sure everyone is fluent with their lines.

In one corner of the ops room set, Steve Bradshaw is supervising the construction of an Artificial Reality platform. The stage hands are actually re-dressing the teleport platform used in last week's episode, painting the letters 'A.R.' on the surface, and constructing a metal railing on three sides. This set will be used tomorrow by Rimmer, Lister and the Cat while they're in the computer game.

Back in the BBC's visual effects workshop, James Davis is putting the finishing touches on the A.R. helmets to be used tomorrow. The costume department will be providing the gloves and boots – several pairs of repainted ski boots are already drying outside the wardrobe department.

Meanwhile, Peter Bates is feverishly editing the footage from Tuesday and Thursday. These scenes, as well as the black-and-white gangster sequence shot last week, will be shown to the studio audience, so their reactions can be added to the final sound mix. With two days' worth of footage to edit, Peter has his work cut out.

Craig is particularly keen to see how his quayside scene with Lorretta comes out: 'It's great to be the one who gets kissed for a change. Why does Rimmer get kissed in every episode of *Red Dwarf*, and I never ever get kissed on the lips? I felt Lister really needed a love interest. He's the only human being left alive, which means that Mr Wiggly has been on bread and water for three million years. I was quite happy to finally have that love scene.'

SATURDAY

The cast starts rehearsing at 10 a.m., with Andy and his cameramen blocking each shot, so everyone is familiar with them by tonight's recording. The rehearsal/camera blocking goes on until lunch time. It's been a hectic week, and traces of fatigue are beginning to show. Robert shows up wearing a pair of opaque black sunglasses to protect his sensitive eyes, and Craig, who's been doing the morning show for Kiss FM for the past three months, is sporting his own pair of translucent blue shades. Of the four cast members, only Danny seems immune to exhaustion.

As the director, cast and cameramen continue with rehearsals, it seems an excellent opportunity to visit the on-site production facilities that have been set up outside the *Red Dwarf* stage. Offering their services as unofficial tour guides through the maze of mixers and microphones are technical manager Jeff Jeffrey, who oversees each aspect of the recording, and vision supervisor Mike Spencer.

The first stop is the lighting cabin, where Dai Thomas spends most of his day shrouded in darkness, monitoring and adjusting the studio lamps. 'Dai's job is to balance the

lamps so they get the right feel,' explains Jeff. 'Because he's responsible for the look of the picture, he needs to be in subdued light, so he can see proper lighting levels. He has two transmission monitors in front of him, which are switchable between each camera, so he can see all the shots. At the moment, Dai is talking to John Pomphrey on the studio floor, who is telling him what he needs to do with the lights. When they've established a balance for each scene, Dai puts it into the memory, so he can call it up when we do that scene.'

On the opposite end of the cabin is the editing suite used by Peter Bates for the weekly pre-edit. '*Red Dwarf* is rather particular, because we do a pre-record day, which has to be cut together to show an audience,' says Jeff. 'The actual cutting of the show is done a week or two later, but we need to get these sequences together to show an

audience. They may not be technically correct, because some shots are still missing, but we try to show something so they can follow the story.'

The next stop is the scanner, where the show's sound and video are recorded. Mike Spencer takes us through the production facilities. 'Basically, the scanner is divided into three areas: production, where the director sits, and an engineering area that's divided into sound and video tape. At the front is Andy the director and Simon the vision mixer. Andy has five screens in front of him, reproducing the output of each camera, and he tells Simon which to cut up on the monitor. Chrissie, the production assistant, reads the script, calls out the shots and furnishes an endless stream of hilarious pornographic innuendo. Simon has access to each of the cameras, as well as the different mix and wipe effects.

'The next bit is vision control,' Mike continues, moving along the van's interior. 'We have control over the iris of the camera, and how the picture actually looks. The cameraman points the camera, zooms and focuses it, but everything else is done here. We can change the sharpness, the exposure, or even the colour.'

Mike indicates the rear of the scanner, where sound man Keith Mayes is working. 'Basically, we've got a 36-channel stereo sound base here. There are different mics for the booms, effects, and for the audience. Keith will mix the show into different groups, so there's a separate track on one of the VTs which is just audience, there's another one which is a mix from the actors, and then there's an overall mix that ultimately goes to the viewers at home. That will be the audience laughter, the actors and the sound effects, which will be dubbed afterwards.'

The tour now completed, Mike leads the way back to

the exit. 'This whole series is shot more like a film,' he comments. 'When you go to the cinema, the lights are out, and you're seeing it under proper viewing conditions. When most people watch television, they've got the lights on, the phones are ringing, and there are all sorts of things happening. We want them to turn all their lights out, and enjoy watching *Red Dwarf* for a half-hour. In the end, that's what all this is for.'

At 3.30 the cast and crew have a 'stagger-through beginning at 9.30'; i.e. a continuous reading of the day's scenes. The visual effects crew has brought in the A.R. helmets, and the artists try them on for size. Looking at these elaborate devices, with their flip-up visors and blinking rays of light, one might almost believe they actually work.

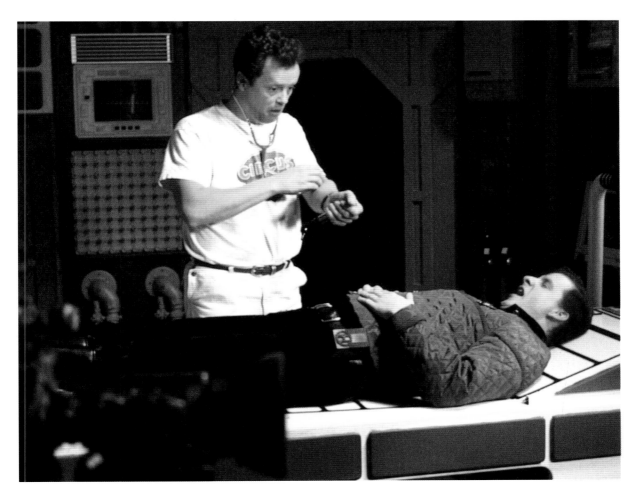

By this time, the computer graphics for the fictional games, Gumshoe and Streets of Laredo, have been routed to the ops room monitor, and Craig and Robert practise with the computer keyboard, as if they are booting up the games themselves. A 'working' medical bed has also been built for the scene where Kryten has contracted the computer virus. 'The idea is that Kryten's liquids will be flowing through it,' says Mel, 'so we had to build a pump into it. There's a car battery that operates the small switches on the front of the bed, and the pump is connected to the main power supply.'

After the stagger-through, Rob and Doug sit down with Andy and the cast members to give final notes to the actors and to discuss with Andy any camera shots they feel don't

work. The meeting is followed by a dress run, and at 5 p.m., Robert goes into make-up to begin the two-hour transformation into Kryten.

At 5.30 p.m. the cast and crew break for dinner, and the stage is cleared for the night's recording. By this time, many of the fans have already arrived at Shepperton, and are socializing in the bar or congregating in the corridor outside Stage G. Many of them have travelled several hours for tonight's taping, coming from as far away as Birmingham, Somerset and Manchester where the series was originally recorded. So far, every taping has been overbooked, and additional chairs have been set up near a

LIMMER
I CREATED THEM. ALL OF THEM.
EVERYONE ON THE PLANET. ALL IN
MY EXACT IMAGE. CAN YOU IMAGINE
A SOCIETY COMPOSED ENTIRELY OF ME?

RIMMER
THOUSANDS UPON THOUSANDS OF BACK-
STABBING TREACHEROUS, HYPOCRITICAL,
COWARDLY, SLIME-MONGERING JUDASES.
THEY OVERTHREW ME, AND WHEN THEY
FOUND OUT THEY COULDN'T DAMAGE MY
HARD LIGHT DRIVE, THEY LOCKED ME IN
HERE, SO I COULD NEVER THREATEN
THEIR INSANE LUST FOR POWER.

monitor outside the stage to handle the overflow crowd.

The audience is admitted at 7 p.m. and by 7.15 Andy Bull, the show's warm-up man, has started his act. Rather than use a comedian as a warm-up, the producers have opted for a variety act, which offers some contrast to *Red Dwarf*'s comedic style.

At 7.30 the cast is introduced to the audience, and the taping is ready to begin. Craig takes his place on the A.R.

platform and slips his helmet on. The monitors play back
the now-edited opening gangster sequence, and the action
cuts back and forth between the pre-taped segments, and
the scenes being recorded live.

Craig and Robert seem to come alive in front of an
audience; ad libbing wildly when one of them blows a line,
and making extremely rude comments between takes. One
of the biggest unscripted laughs of the night occurs during

a retake of Thursday's final scene. Danny and Craig are lying across a table in Starbug's mid-section, with Robert standing over them holding a video camera. Looking down and seeing Craig's head near his nether regions, Robert quips, 'As long as you're down there . . .' It's one joke that will never make it to the small screen.

EPILOGUE

With blinding speed, Starbug plunges towards the surface of the bubbling lava planet, only moments away from total destruction. Inside the ship, the four crew members burst into the cockpit, and Kryten begins loading the computer program that will restore navigational control to them.

'How long will it take?' shouts Rimmer.

'Just a few seconds,' replies Kryten, feverishly typing the last few comments. 'How long to impact?'

'Just a few seconds!'

The final sequence is initiated, and the computer clicks on. 'There it goes; I've released it into the navicomp,' announces Kryten. But is it too late? As Starbug burns through the atmosphere, the rest of the crew counts down the last remaining seconds.

Five ... four ... three ... two ... 'We're not going to make it!' cries Lister, as the ship crashes into a sea of lava and disappears. Silence. Only a few bubbles of bursting gas break the surface.

Suddenly, Starbug emerges from the molten sea, its hull in flames. Picking up speed, it climbs into the sky at a dizzying angle. Inside the ship, the crew watch the planet recede beneath them, and join in a triumphant chorus of 'YEE-HAH!'

Now out of danger, the ship heads into space. A blazing sun is setting on the horizon, and as Starbug heads into the sunset, one can almost hear the distinctive sounds of a honky tonk piano playing the final tune. For the crew of Red Dwarf, it's the end of an adventure – and the start of many more.

Back in the real world of Shepperton Studios, the fans begin filtering out of the bar to start their long trek home, and the cast and crew finish a last quick pint before returning to work. There are lines to be learned, make-up tables to be cleaned off, and costumes waiting to be put away. The tangle of cables that cover the floor of Stage G are coiled up and carefully stored for next week. Rocket and his team of cameramen pack up their equipment in special carrying cases, which are stacked near the door to be picked up. One by one, like dimming red and blue suns, John Pomphrey's lights are switched off, leaving a momentary glow and then nothing.

With another episode of *Red Dwarf* finally taped, the crew get into their cars, and slowly file out of Shepperton Studios. At this hour, there's no sunset to head into, but tomorrow will bring a new day, a new set of adventures – and another episode of *Red Dwarf*...

The cast and crew of
Red Dwarf VI

All prices are approximate at date of publication.

CLOTHING

There are over twenty-five styles and designs of Virgin Megastore and HMV best-selling RED DWARF T-shirts and polo shirts, as well as baseball caps, ski hats, melton and leather-sleeved jackets and surf jams. Approx. prices are: T-shirts £10, polo shirts £12.99, melton jackets £60, leather-sleeved jackets £90, base-ball caps and hats £6–10, surf jams £15.

Merchandise is on sale at C & A stores, Milletts, John Cheatle, Virgin Megastores, Our Price and HMV stores nationwide as well as at Forbidden Planet and other sci-fi and independent outlets. The full range of RED DWARF clothing is also available through Distribution Network's mail order service PO Box 10, London SW19 3TW (Tel.: 081 540 5545).

MODEL KITS

KRYTEN (30cm high, six-part plastic model kit which may be posed prior to final assembly) and STARBUG (30cm long) are available in 700 toy and model shops across the UK, including the Beatties chain, as well as through sci-fi and comic shops nationwide. Retail price £37.95 each. The kits are also available through mail order from Sevans Models, PO Box 34, Trowbridge, Wiltshire BA14 8XY.

GREETING CARDS

A wide range of greeting cards for all occasions (approx. price £1.10) is on sale through W.H. Smith, Boots, John Menzies, Clinton Cards, Hallmark, the student market through NUS, other independent outlets and Distribution Network's mail order service (details as above).

POSTERS

RED DWARF posters (size 27" × 39", retail price £3.99) are distributed by Scandecor International and are available in all regular poster outlets including Woolworths, Athena, Asda, Menzies and Forbidden Planet, as well as through Distribution Network's mail order service (details as above).

NOVELS

Infinity Welcomes Careful Drivers (Penguin, £4.99) – an international bestseller penned by Grant Naylor in 1989.

Better Than Life (Penguin, £4.99) – the not-very-long-awaited sequel to *Red Dwarf*. The crew are trapped in the ultimate computer game: Better Than Life. The zenith of computer game technology, BTL transports you directly to a perfect world of your imagination, a world where you can enjoy fabulous wealth and unmitigated success. It's the ideal game with only one drawback – it's so good, it will kill you.

Red Dwarf Omnibus (Penguin, £7.99) – one enormous volume containing the first two RED DWARF novels, *Infinity* and *Better Than Life,* with unmissable new material (including the first draft of the TV pilot scripts and the beer mat on which the original idea was first scribbled).

OTHER BOOKS

Primordial Soup (Penguin, £4.99) – features a selection of the least worst scripts from the first five years of RED DWARF, tracing the series from its humble beginnings to its humble present.

The Official Red Dwarf Companion (Titan, £6.99) – more fun than a year in stasis, more useful than a crochet hat and tastier than a Pot Noodle.

The Red Dwarf Programme Guide (Virgin, £4.99) – all the answers to thousands of vital pieces of information about RED DWARF as seen on television.

The Man in the Rubber Mask (Penguin, £4.99) – actor, alternative comedian and some-time nude model, Robert Llewellyn was plucked from the heights of fame by the unstoppable forces of Grant Naylor and reborn as the robotic Kryten. The inside story of a life spent encased in a latex rubber mask in the BBC special effects department in darkest Acton.

AUDIO BOOKS

Red Dwarf – Infinity Welcomes Careful Drivers is brilliantly narrated and characterized by Chris 'Rimmer' Barrie. The audio book is available as a double cassette (abridged) priced £7.49 and as a six cassette (unabridged) set priced £24.99 in book shops, record shops and garage forecourt shops across the UK. *Better Than Life,* the audio book, is coming soon. For more details write to Laughing Stock Productions Ltd, PO Box 408, London SW11 6JJ.

VIDEOS

The Universe will never be the same again. The original series of RED DWARF has now been released on video. Never repeated on television and not previously available, series 1 is contained on two videos. Also available are series 2, 3 and 4 (each series contained on two cassettes), and in Spring 1994 series 5 is scheduled for release. All are available for only £12.99 each from all good video outlets.

BBCV 4914 Red Dwarf I: *The End*
BBCV 4915 Red Dwarf I: *Confidence and Paranoia*
BBCV 4749 Red Dwarf II: *Krypton*
BBCV 4750 Red Dwarf II: *Stasis Leak*
BBCV 4769 Red Dwarf III: *Backwards*
BBCV 4707 Red Dwarf III: *Timeslides*
BBCV 4847 Red Dwarf IV: *Camille*
BBCV 4848 Red Dwarf IV: *Dimension Jump*

FAN CLUBS

There are currently five official fan clubs and two affiliated clubs.

UK: Red Dwarf Fan Club, 40 Pitford Road, Woodley, Reading, Berkshire RG5 4QF. Send SAE for details

USA: *East Coast:* 1409 West, 14 Mile Road, Madison Heights, Michigan 48071; *West Coast:* PO Box 50552, Palo Alto, California 94303

AUSTRALIA: PO Box 1044, Bundoora, Victoria 3083

IRELAND: 52 Granville Road, Dun Laoghaire, Co. Dublin

AFFILIATED CLUBS: *Germany:* BetterThan Life, z.Hd. Sylvia Prannga Isoldekurz-Str 145(36), Munster-Nienberge; *New Zealand:* Zed Shift, PO Box 10104, Wellington